Awaken To Your Dream

Sir Q

Dedication

To the Father & Ancestors.

Acknowledgments

The thought before the thought is who I am thankful to first (The Father).

- I am thankful for the guidance my soul tribe felt and seen in me even without appearing near me.
- I want to thank Pantheon Publishers, along with my team for the belief, support, acknowledgement, opportunity, and dedication in the assist of awakening all to their dream.
- I want to thank my Pops, for the words of wisdom, love, and always reminding me that I can do anything I put my mind to.
- I want to thank Ma, for showing/giving love even to a kid that she didn't birth yet showing that it doesn't take such an action for someone to be family.
- I want to thank my siblings, for showing and informing me of what type of life I want for myself. Even when it didn't always seem clear.
- I want to thank my friends/acquaintances, for the belief of potential that they saw in me along with the encouragement of this gift.

About the Author

Sir Q is a passionate writer and poet whose work embodies wisdom, joy, and the pursuit of peace. Having grown up experiencing the extremes of life while standing in the middle, Sir Q's writing reflects a deep understanding of life's complexities. With each poem, he strives to spread love and laughter, connecting with readers through his raw, honest truth.

His words often reflect a journey of self-discovery, resilience, and the power of inner strength. Whether in moments of joy or sorrow, Sir Q believes in standing firm in the face of adversity, using writing as a means to inspire others to do the same. His work resonates with those seeking guidance, understanding, or simply a connection to something greater. Sir Q continues to share his journey with the world, looking toward the future and the endless possibilities that await.

Stepping into Consciousness

Shattered Stardom

You could have had it all, like a shooting star,

But instead, you stand appalled, looking at the wall,

Wishing upon that star, if only, if only,

One would've never let you fall.

Yes, could've had it all, like the mall.

But now, you're stuck in the pain—

No, let's say the fame,

'Cause now it's such a shame

That you ain't in this picture frame.

Thinking it was a game,

Started out as the grain,

Now that slice is your pain,

Never knowing how to explain.

Even without pointing the finger,

Still, you're the one to blame.

Don't feel ashamed—just put your name in the game,

Leave them lames in the dirt, knowing it's all kind of the same.

All they do is hurt, being far from the main.

Girl, please, just use your brain!

So go ahead and call something like your main,

Maybe even your Gucci Mane,

Could govern the whole state,

Yes, giving you the shining state.

Have you looking so spectacular in the face,

Something like an extravagant vase.

Closet Confessions

If you don't want to talk to me, then why stalk me?

If you don't want to fuck with me, then why screw with me?

It's like you're the opposite, and you've got me trapped in this closet,

Dark, and don't see any, call that Stevie.

Gave you chances, you can even say plenty.

Gave you many ounces of love, ridicule.

Oh, it is my drug, call it critical.

Indeed, it's starting to fall beneath you.

Don't even know why it couldn't be seen within you,

Like being in an accident and trapped in these four doors.

It's ancient in the past, just open your corridor.

Knowing we can make this last,

With no need for a college class.

Let's just talk this over with a glass of wine.

Man, the knowledge flows like a glass of time.

Call it an hourglass, 'cause you're finer than a glass of wine.

Honeyed Farewell

Yeah, you're my honey, can even call you my sweet bee,

But I have to let you go, to continue making this money and be me!

Acting like life isn't reality, but it's just so free—

So why sit and play me like the damn enemy?

My lady, just remember me, hoping it hurts when thinking of me,

Wishing these thoughts would just flee from this memory,

Knowing you ain't Ashanti, yet still so into me.

Baby, just get with me, and maybe it will be shown, this epiphany.

So in love, definitely, even drop the drug mentally and physically.

Gave you so much trust, and for that, I was hurt the worst.

Yes! Missing your touch, seemingly always gave me a rush.

Go ahead, crack a smile, knowing joy is what makes you blush.

Thinking of making you into a bust, meaning transcending above this lust—

Nothing like iron, so no need to think of the rust.

Shh, hush that fuss, and like a volcano erupting, yes, here comes the bust!

Darling, let's just get rid of all this dust,

And if it must be, only spelling this bee once.

Maze of Restraint

Her mind is going through a daze,

She's blind, like going through a maze.

Damn, she makes it so easy to explain,

It's like her own name is what's restrained.

But bet you're the one to blame with your pain,

Now being stuck with the lame.

Spent so much time together, even gave you your favorite nicknames,

Not hearing any proclaims.

Never had to walk in shame, knowing that it was never a game.

Even at the beginning, started etching you into the brain.

Looking back, it must not have been tamed,

Allowing you to come and take this flame.

Knowing you're not the same, even though you became the Great Dane.

So, by taking aim and exclaiming you'll never inflame this grand dame the same again,

While being stuck in this picture frame, and damn, it's getting bigger—

Then what can be configured?

Like a senior star stuck in fame,

Yet still never fail to remember your name.

Mirrored Silence

Feeling no attachments, like a wireless phone,

Making you feel speechless, so you mirror how it feels on your own.

Now, trying to seek this, has you so confused—sit down so one can leak this.

Her favorite color is pink, that's one trying to link this.

Being in an alloyed state, call it something like zinc.

So don't even put this one in the sink,

Knowing being cleaner than the dishes.

Always taking chances, so no need for making wishes.

Still feeling so stressful, but if you listen, you can tell this rhyme is so senseful.

Never meaning to diss ya,

Just wanting to let you know I still miss ya.

How about letting one still be your best kisser?

No need for a net, nor trying to make a bet,

One's already fished ya, just wanted you to realize this picture.

Houdini's Truth

Why do these lames walk around like they're just so untamed?

Always proud as hell, it's time to show just how one feels.

Never walk in shame, and for that, always retained my name.

Call it Houdini, put the name in the box, it comes out golden.

Ain't he?!

Well, he ain't no Henry, no, not nearly.

Saying maybe he ain't real, so go ahead and put him on the heel.

Yeah, that's the bottom of the shoe, so the feeling must be kind of blue.

His world is cold, he's sick, so it's something like the flu.

Blazed! Eyes hazy, you know they stuck close, call it crazy glue.

Should've seen it in his eyes, that was the first clue.

Even heard it in the voice but believed it couldn't be true.

That was the last mistake, never making another.

Even without a mother, treated you as a brother.

And all you made it do is crumble, like a dog in a muzzle.

Tumbling through this desert, even the weeds want to be green.

Something like a tumbleweed in this lifelike puzzle.

Already fell into the puddle, knowing you don't exist.

Please don't even try to risk it, already dismissed ya.

Won't even miss ya, so please paint a vivid fucking picture.

Angel's Insight

Doing this fresh, like a test on the mind,

Best believe, I'm on the grind.

Always stretching time past the hills that have eyes,

Now seeing stars in everyone's lives.

Don't be ashamed, we are on the same side.

Smile! Loving the way it shines,

Like a white dove soaring through these bright skies.

Go ahead, knowing you can fly, you're an angel.

Walking by, you make legs light and feel tranquil.

Having no equal, you're like a perfect vessel.

Just really wanting some blessings, ma'am.

Look what they're selling, rum.

Well, come, let's make an item, hun,

With this seldom sanctum,

Something like a Kingdom... Come!

Even curing any symptoms,

Spitting so much wisdom.

So, blow. A lil' Khalif.

Roll with a bit of beliefs,

And then start to chief on this Greenleaf.

But just for a brief, still trying to finish this speech.

Knowing you're going to call 11:30 that's foresight,

That's when you're by yourself and wanting company all night.

You know it ends just right… in the moonlight.

Call us insomniacs, we be up... through twilight.

Pier of Destiny

We had so many pastimes, but the one

That's being looked for was the one that came before.

Treating you like my last dime,

Missing you, like a missing roof on the pigeon coop.

Here, take the scoop, just here for the truth,

Even without the damn group,

Girl, keep one in the loop,

Down to be a trooper,

Expressing how you're so damn super!

Yeah, this is a future stay, call it your wedding day,

Making it so one never pays, or even so we won't delay.

Not trying to go home, just simply trying to propose,

Telling you the words you wanted to hear,

Even on the dark and lonely pier.

Telling you "I do," even when one didn't conclude.

No, it wasn't being rude; stop being so crude.

Making things look like fantasy,

But taking this hand will emit your destiny.

Destiny, take your destiny, and please just take the best of me.

Like one said, this ain't no fantasy, so baby, just dance with me.

Karmic Bloom

Yes, it's kinda scary... The words that one fiddles on this paper

Are getting heavy; it even comes true.

Bet, it doesn't have to be a full moon

To see its true bloom, something like the close goon!

But now, seeing the past will never last.

What goes around comes around, call that shit karma.

But coming from one, yeah, it's a bunch of drama.

Stressing, one already knows, ask Father God for some blessings.

Resting, pulling these dreads, don't know what to do,

Racing the brain, clearly not insane,

Already cut the hair, don't even need a dare.

Patiently waiting on this life, and for you to care,

Instead of being pulled like a chicken on a piece of string.

That's why you will never get this ring.

Inventory of Love

Showed how to love, even showed how to hate.
Take this hand, sweet pee, and we'll be forever straight.
No, let's say forever great —
like we're smoking on them sweet trees by the Great Salt Lake.

You have an amazing imagination, just don't mistake it with reality,
cause then it'll be a brutality, maybe even a fatality.
Yes, it's a crazy combination, but don't let the next step be your
abomination.

Walking into this life, just wanting to protect what's called the wife,
but while glaring at that picture frame, thinking we're all the same,
yet trying to inform that one's nothing like 'em,
leaving it at that, with nothing left to blame.

Look into these eyes — why so ashamed?
It's like a maimed heart, and it's gotten so restrained.
Come unto me, sweetheart, relieving all the pain.
A true love story that can be taken to the glory,
always keeping it in heart — call it the inventory.

Rhymes & Wine

Sticking to the lines and memorizing the rhymes,

'cause it doesn't take nothing but a dime of time.

Even take her out for a glass of that wine,

but she likes it better in the room — that's where the dine is real fine.

Finer than some rice, never have a price.

She keeps me adjacent to her Nikes, while treating her just right,

staying close, like a string on a kite.

Nothing like acquaintances, wanting me all night.

Something like Achilles' heel,

but never falling, won't even fucking kneel,

even if hit on the heel.

Don't even reconsider — just come and be the sitter.

We'll cruise to the tomb, but before these lips lock,

one's stating, "You're stunning like the moon,

never to meet your doom, even when in a bad mood.

Please just watch the previews, knowing one's coming soon."

Divine Proof

Always speaking the truth, like loving the way faces light up —
hmm... fireflies.

So, don't try and fly away; these are no lies, they will never sly away.

Yes, it's time to harken, so make it easier and start barking.

Saying, "I am the truth," but like the evidence at a crime scene,

always looking for a clue — start believing this walking proof.

Didn't even give us the time to let our minds bind,

not even an effort to let our love combine.

Feeling as though one's coming from the heavens, yes, so divine.

Been together on this dateline for a quiet eternity;

makes sense why our blood is so confined.

This bloodline will never be a deadline,

so go ahead, sit in the Lazy Boy, and just recline.

Wildfire Passion

It's getting harder to sleep,

tossing and turning, just free-falling through these sheets.

Somebody spare a hand to find a way up out these creeks.

See, the passion being seeked is in these rhymes that speak.

It's like my rhymes are my session, still reluctant to even peek,

but the brain is starting to leak, just like the gasoline on the street.

It made a ring around this life, so upon lighting that burning ring of fire,

to meet the girl most desired! Having no time for a liar liar,

just come and be the burning fire — something like a wildfire,

while reminding one of a sapphire.

Open the ears and listen for the one who's really admired.

Believe in thyself while preaching the truth,

like a priceless gem, always striving to acquire the proof.

Extravagant Ascent

Model of the year — that is a true story.

It gets purer with every shedding tear; go ahead, ask Corey. Forever this star is soaring, but most like it better when one starts touring.

Yes, this car is foreign, and this new witch is getting kinda boring. Upon showing the dotted line, the past begins mourning.

Never trying to exaggerate, only here to elaborate.

Open your eyes! Look, it's an extravagant date! These dreads are getting longer, like how the bank account is stretching further.

This energy flows like a waterfall, stacking inner-chi taller than Niagara Falls.

Just come and be a nagging call, while showing how I bag it all.

Lionhearted Circle

Yes, got the heart of a lion — no, not lying, man.

Just use your inspiration, with more determination.

Won't even see another hater's motivation,

showing strength — call it Arnold Schwarzenegger!

Resonate on what is said, my little Terminator!

By turning the other cheek, becoming your own savior.

Death crawling down this field, just trying to get to 50,

or should it be said, the beauty? Yes, we want the trophy.

So do another 50, and hold it up like its holy,

bearing all this weight, so never tell oneself you can't.

Call it the circle of life, continuing this road — oh yes, until the afterlife!

Coming from so much strife, looking at this hand holding the knife.

Never been a lowlife, continue living the high life —

it can be said one adores the nightlife.

Beauty's Apex

Yes, you are the beauty, inspired to make a new duty.

Saying you're something like a cutie, but for now let's get loony.

Just come and be a sitter, nowhere near close to bitter.

But even being sour, remain knowing how to wield power.

Nothing like a downer — yes, that smile keeps one higher.

Plus, the light blue skies remind one of those light blue eyes,

watching one just soar through these night-light skies.

But only if you're right by my side — got the feeling that one can glide.

Let's not get on the way; we gaze into each other's eyes.

It's like we're trapped up in a maze, with our brains going through a change,

knowing clearly not insane, due to the fact you remember the name.

The way you walk is so mesmerizing, urging others to start visualizing.

Stand tall and start realizing, that thyself is the one that will never fall.

Something like a recent call, so come unto thee, my magnificent doll.

Dreamscape Chill

Hey, it's so cold — it's not just a world.

This is another world, so cold it couldn't be fathomed.

It is getting harder to come into your dreams, even when imagined.

But with understanding that we dream fast,

obtain the freshness like a test on the mind,

knowing we are the best team of the past.

Even if it didn't last, we still had a blast.

Harken to the words so one can orchestrate these rhymes.

Don't want to see a soul continue walking around Stevie blind.

We were just teens — it wasn't your fault.

Stay up on your feet; don't let them lock you in the vault.

Heard you're seeing a shrink — well,

he's going to help you get past this brink.

Just pay attention to what links,

never making you feel like the weakest link.

But staring so hard, relentless to even blink!

Showing the signs to get by this little chink,

but having us all fooled — it can even be said, hoodwinked.

It seems that being used like a tool has turned you into a fool.

Seasons of Us

Only had her for the spring,
even though it's just the beginning, she's already asking for the ring.

In the summer, yea, she warmer,
but she is still my newcomer.

In the fall, we stand taller,
'cause we love to ball harder.

However, in winter,
she overcomes getting bitter.
Just call on me to be your new sitter.
Never say never — being in this life, yo, that's forever.

Hurling these haters to the bottom of the sea, like. An. Anchor.
That being known as a demotion, giving one another promotion.
Streaming the motion within the ocean, just like a coachman.
Heeding the little cautions always makes for better options.

Like how, being through so much strife in this life of time,
makes one consider finding a wife in this life to dine.

Theraflu Flow

Yea, the favorite color is blue.

Now, calling me something like the flu,

my words are the Theraflu,

and as it's said, they are the cure.

This flow is going outrageous; keep up to find what's new.

Just listen to this Theraflu.

But this verse might just punish you, yes, just seen you vanish too.

So, go ahead and start raising the bar,

even from the dead, still shooting like a star.

These bars are growing in this vision,

managing all this broken tension.

Yes, even more than what's in a prison,

but it seems as though it's provoking this living.

Doing this since these thoughts are vivid,

have you living life, just so livid,

while spending time on the mind,

even money, while on the grind,

spending it all in this life of mine,

while making it in this lifetime.

Knowing the way around the crime,

that's when one went and copped a nine.

Yea, go and get it, harnessing energy,

while moving hands like Father Time.

Break it down, spread some synergy,

now preparing the damn remedy.

White Walls

White wall, white walls,

that's all one sees in these bright halls.

Running and never stopping until night falls,

but even without the right call.

See, just looking to acquire the proof,

quit messing with the head, 'cause one desires truth.

Stay admiring the swag, that's why this being is in a suit.

Continuation of replenishing health, so you can cop a coupe.

On the verge of diminishing your wealth, by spreading a bit of loot.

This is about to be a calamity, or even a catastrophe,

so quit thinking about the fantasy.

Ongoing, to change this future drastically,

expressing, this is the destiny, nothing like Maybelline.

So just take the best of me,

never conforming to counterfeit, always having the stylish fit.

Stay rocking the flyest shit, that just means one's the biggest hit.

But even marching to fame, the heart appears maimed,

unto me the perfect soul, so it's never full of pain.

While we all still see white walls, white walls,

pacing through these bright halls.

Call for Ruth

Mary three times,

while in this state of mind.

That means this world was cold,

just call it a life of crime.

To survive in this world, some got to be shown,

then have the nerve to become more bold.

Yes, a real one, they are always being told,

and you know only the real ones are who get chosen.

Appearing to do this all alone, momma passed as a youngster.

That means a part will forever be dead and gone,

like breathing without a lung.

Taking it all to the head, yea, it's my zone.

Please, momma, come back home.

Being in so much disbelief,

watching the previews of this life, and my mind starts to roam.

Starting to roll up all the beliefs, giving another Greenleaf

to make the heart chrome.

With no hesitation, following the feeling to this location,

blessed with a silver tongue, that's just for communication.

Making this the obligation,

to never stop until we reach salvation.

Now that's called teaching determination without a physical patient.

That's why one's dividing anyone in the way, just to lace it,

showing all how to embrace it, reminiscing on how we are ancient.

Now thinking of going to the knight's table, ecstatically, it's the opposite of vacant.

Fortune's Favor

Yea, got the knowledge,

just acknowledge the dollar accumulation.

Yea, this money talks, can even say it has communication skills.

Now, time to take it on a date,

soaring over some of the great lakes.

Hurry up, don't want to miss the wake and bake.

Yea, you know we're nothing close to fake,

bet we're on the uplift, try again and get a facelift,

while going faster than a foreign car.

Yea, we know that's kinda bizarre,

but one is higher than the flying fortress.

Just try and take my dying fortune,

then it will be shown that you could never torch it.

Payday Manifesto

Yea, speak the mind, so you can be an understander.

They all huddle around, like some bystanders,

needing to stand by, still setting standards.

That means whipping the pie,

but go ahead, make 'em lie, or should it be said, lay?

'Cause we're about to make them pay,

yes, live life every day, like it is payday.

Since being separated at birth,

that means it's nothing to be decimated from the earth.

Yo, these rhymes linger, can even say they hurt.

Even being so damn eager, that nothing will be left in the dirt.

Only some can conjure up a glimpse of what one ponders.

By the time they start marching up, we're already over yonder.

Thinking three moves ahead,

while some still trying to get out of the bed.

Seeing that body is full of lead, some just had to suffer,

showing in their world, one's far from being a bluffer.

No, don't mutter, we are already tougher.

Go ahead, we don't stutter, slicing through the lies like butter.

Bionic Rise

Knowledge grows like being bionic,

going faster, call that super sonic.

Graduated from no college, just listen to some logic,

being the topic of discussion,

fire breathing, while they are trapped up in a dungeon.

Don't even give their ass a chance to start purging,

'cause we. Never! Stop surging.

That's how some turned into a Persian,

and others fell on the table of a surgeon.

See, look here, kinda ruthless, but never clueless.

Keeping these hands clean, go ahead, call it selfish.

Yes, keep that currency, that makes some want to come home with me.

Thought one told, these rhymes are lethal,

grabbing for another single, while reaching another sequel.

So, let's go toe to toe, let's go, let's mingle.

Proceed with caution, one has no equal.

Sticky Magic

They call us something like the cutie and the beast,

but being my beauty in the sheets,

while we are getting silly in the streets.

Calling me crazy Q, she said main character too,

picking up these P's & Q's,

shocking, these other people too.

Sit back and start to realize

that we are stacking up what shines.

Yes, they are lyrically inclined, decalcifying the eye.

She gets better with age, so she's finer than wine.

When she is on the mind, that's when she is going to page,

being on the grind, then one turns into a mage.

That means turnt magic, now conversing without the static,

nothing like Pinky and the Brain, but it's sticky, yet still sane.

Flight to Neverland

Just fly away to the meet, yea, call it Peter Pan,

taken wherever the heart desires, even Never Never Land.

Since we're flying together to see, admiring how we can hear the bands,

check the gauge, keep the change, yea, it sounds kinda strange.

Just hop in the Range, then we'll explain.

Never treating thee like a creature, really loving the amazing features,

oblige, while one takes you out to breakfast, showing you how to manifest this.

Stretching these thoughts like a bungee cord, they will always catch, however much the load,

like a blue flame while in a blue T, still knowing thyself as the beauty.

Silent Bob's Court

Smoking on Silent Bob, at least that's what it's called,

going up for a quiet lob, just explaining how to always ball,

hand all in the face, still going for a jump shot,

in the process of counting big banks, 'cause some ain't even get a jumpstart.

Yea, it's all net, like we always had a bet,

concentrating on the rim, contemplating on how the lights are getting dim.

Only when one is meditating, being in a true film,

now their money is getting slimmer, while doing things so timidly.

Mine, still growing bigger, stop comparing to end living life so lividly.

No comprehension on what one is making, so paint this picture vividly,

making about 10 figures, knowing this finger stays on the trigger,

calling me the eye of the tiger, doing my shit religiously,

rocking with this beat, while they debate on who meets.

Still sitting in the seat, passing time playing with the anomaly,

seeing us rolling in a Phantom, call it Green Lantern,

only needing one ring, that bling-blings,

'cause the feeling in this heart is urging to help these fiends.

Distraction Revue

Always been your distraction,

On the verge of making a movie, oh yea, that means action.

So don't make a sound, already feeling the intention of the reaction.

We are something like math, but don't only embrace the subtraction.

Treating ye like a wildflower, even before arriving on the Mayflower.

Seeing all this gun smoke powder, knowing one shouldn't give out all their power.

It will help you stand prouder, working out these kinks, striving to find the perfect link.

Yes, it's your dream, take a double blink,

Knowing all these diamonds are really gleaming.

Seeing past the spectrum of this light prism,

Look at all the stars steady beaming, who needs a golden bar?

One is finally rested, to see the true vision.

Listen to what is said; that means pay attention.

Never failing to mention, this is done with no tension.

Pain's Embrace

Go ahead and start to kill 'em with the pain,

Driving in your own lane, smoking on plain Jane,

Leaving all the vampires dying in the rain,

Failing to remember the name.

Now that one drained all the pain away,

All up in the stars, yea, even saying the fame,

Knowing you were the kissing beauty,

Staying in the street, just for you to have a place to eat.

Still never trusting fully,

While wearing the lust of a goddess,

As they're starting to rust, the emergence of someone the hottest.

From top to bottom, knowing it's spotless,

From bottom to top, can even say lawless.

When our grips are united, we're so damn flawless,

Ill intent, begone from this blessing.

Knowing one has the quickest draw,

Seems like we'll have to teach 'em, like a college lesson.

Go ahead and cool, like a bowl of coleslaw,

Knowing one has no flaw, too bad you drew the shortest straw.

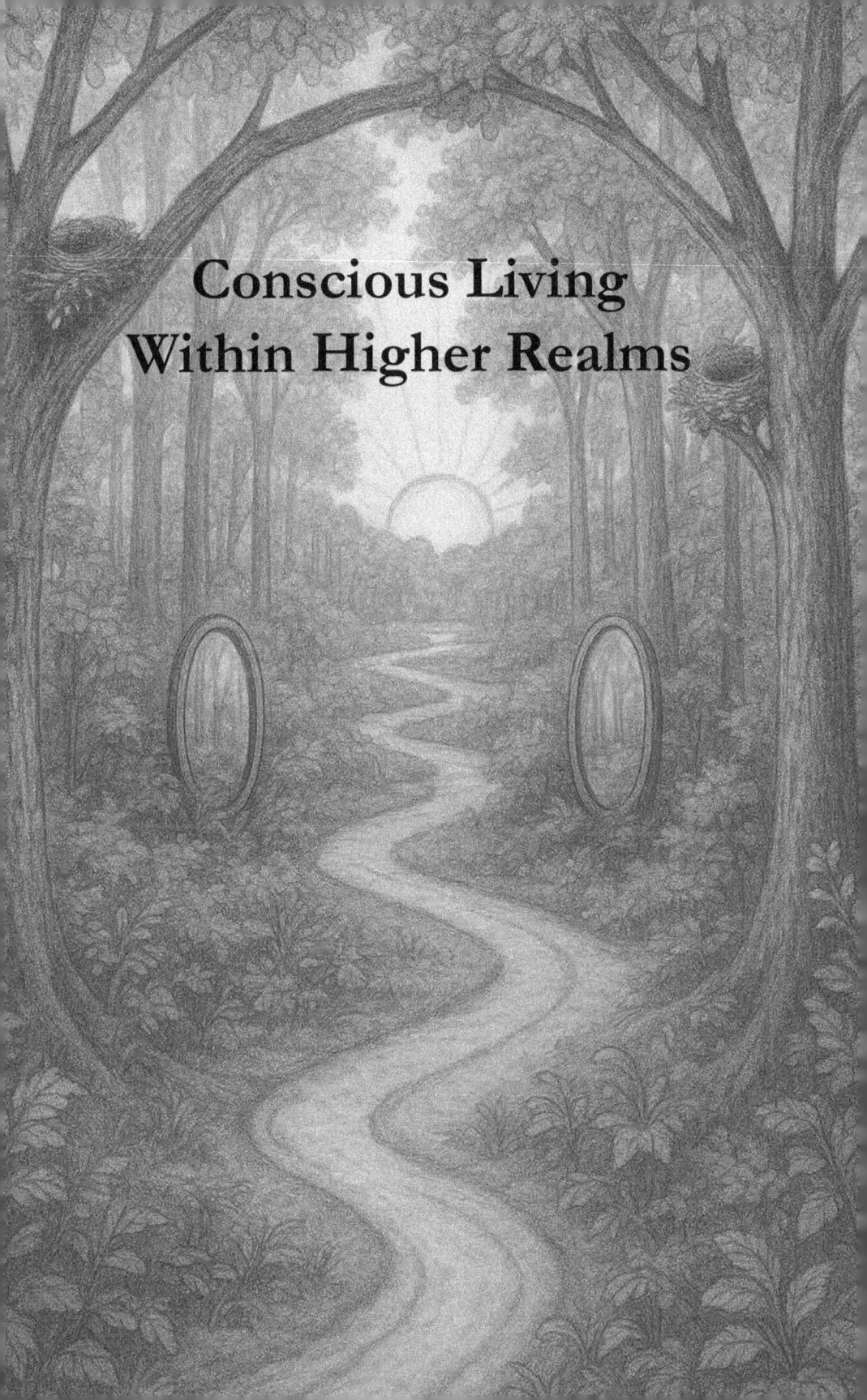

Conscious Living Within Higher Realms

Divine Soul-dier

Back when one ain't have shit,

You left because one wasn't the biggest hit.

But now, being rich and famous,

Got you so livid that you're going to be left nameless.

Staying higher than a bumblebee,

Come on, staying high even off the humble trees,

Giving a vivid picture to reconcile the enemies.

Keep your friends close, and enemies closer;

No, this life will never come to a closure.

Seeing one standing taller than a toy soldier,

I am a Divine Soul-dier,

Got 'em mimicking the style like a parrot on a shoulder.

Could've stayed by this side, now you're left in Canada, where we know it gets colder.

Please escuchan, thought one damn told ya, being the mistake that had to take.

So, while we're trying to wake and bake, yet still worried about acting fake,

Knowing it's nothing but a shake away for one to explore the ways to make them pay.

Arcane Mastery

Yes, got the static with it, go ahead and page thee.

Told you that one's magic with it, meaning like a mage be.

They looking in the past like it was shellshock,

But just mad at how fast these dreads locked.

That means wisdom is coming faster,

Sit and ponder while writing this speech.

Yes, got to preach it, like I am the pastor!

Or even a master of disguise,

But the next step might be a disaster through your eyes.

Stay looking for the right colors, and still so mesmerized.

Blackjack, flapjack, still flipping out, flipping cards and flipping dimes,

Staying on the guard until called to die.

That means that black hearse is pulling up; never will it burst into flames,

Unless trying to figure out the difference between these two lanes.

That's just the way the game goes, and if you're walking by, don't forget to pay the toll.

But never willing to fold — all to do is hold thy own.

Oh yea, all in, call that shit a full house, 'cause we are about to pull out,

Steady rocking with the main lady, as she's telling everybody, "That is my baby!"

V6 to G6

Speeding in the max, doing it to the Maxima.

Yeah, it's a V6, but let's exchange it with this G6.

Yeah, all the cameras trying to take a quick pic,

But you know, we slick with it.

At the crib watching Netflix, pouring all the greatest liq.

Have you been thinking you're in your latest marriage?

How about showing you a barrage?

Low kick to the chin, in time to meet the end,

So go ahead and tell Mother Hen.

They couldn't even blend your face to look above average;

That bruised you so good, calling me the savage.

Just so crucial that you took my 'O' away from me,

Talking about Ophelia, now look who's screaming Nina.

This will probably bleed ya, just rehydrate yourself,

Sip more Aquafina — this happened just after Hurricane Katrina.

Fraternal Flame

Yes, having the eternal pain, come and see this fraternal flame,

Speak it and write it, now leaking it, and it makes them want to riot.

And since they eating it up, the obvious remedy is to diet,

Don't fight it, just buy it, beat beating up, clean — cleaner than Mr. Clean.

Call it something like Trident, while striding all the way to the top,

Meaning riding with pride, all the way to paradise,

Dying on a perceived lonely road, then they throw the rice.

Help me roll the dice, seeing it's more my destiny

When you want to walk the life of Christ,

So we don't have to witness another calamity.

Pegasus Dreams

One got you over there fantasizing

About how these rhymes can be so paralyzing.

Even when the lights are out, the fam always told, "Don't doubt, pull out."

No, not from Vegas, still feeling higher like Pegasus.

Not trying to fall out, maybe just ball out,

That's why one is chilling with Grandaddy, blowing on that Grandaddy,

While pouring knowledge in thy cup,

So one's not in the game looking oh so sloppy or rough.

Can even say he raised me up from a pup,

Quite similar to mine, which is his mentality.

The ill intent you keep projecting at thee

Has Channel 13 examining another fatality.

Go ahead, dash away, triggering anxiety,

Call on Vash, the stampede.

Forget about letting you leave, especially if you made him bleed.

Go ahead, take another shot, so one can help you believe.

Only taking a chain or the clock — now watch them all flee.

Just read what's on the sleeve; not talking about the shirt,

It's these scars on the arm — fool, please.

Toxic Swag

While improving your style shopping at Hot Topic,

This swag keeps evolving, 'cause it's close to damn toxic.

Why don't you just vox it?

Bet the mouthpiece is just so logic.

Of course! Because of smoking on this, everybody is calling chronic,

Helping to write, even think.

Hot dog! It even helps some get through the day.

Gloating on the court, yet come meet the humble me,

Floating in a ring like a butterfly,

And still stinging like a bumblebee.

Never sly-ing away from me — call it Muhammad Ali,

Doing what must be done, putting these haters behind me,

Just like a cool breeze.

When walking by, one makes people want to stop and freeze.

Shaded Destiny

Sitting in the shade, you can tell one is cooling,

Looking through these L.O.C.s — yeah, just fooling.

These girls are still screaming over Mother Nature,

Just inhaling all the air while engulfing all these lines of hearing you say you care.

Already know if you ride, we will prevail,

Talking about playing truth or dare.

While looking at your face, it seems so pale,

Just take this hand, so we can live life so damn swell.

Hearing the remains of the bell, something like a wedding day,

Allow one to continue guiding you to your destiny, never seeing the saddest day.

Yup, like the baddest blade, being something like a keeper,

But start trying to be a seeker — then prepare for me to freak ya,

Doing this oh so typical,

But bet it's just so meaningful — let's not make this anything political,

While grasping all the truths with something like a tentacle.

Scholarly Stage

Sitting at the top, no need for a hostage,

About to pop the collar, showing how to drop some knowledge,

On the stage with all these scholars,

Striving and already graduating from the college,

Showing how to stack up all these dollars.

Living the college life, while others keep passing out,

Could've shown how to play the fife,

But couldn't play your cards right.

My rhymes are rife with all these damn stories,

Taking in so much emotion that the eyes start getting blurry.

Being something like Jet Li, had to show the fury,

They better tread carefully before they unleash me,

Meaning he might relinquish thee until shivering tremendously.

That's just the morning announcement — hints to the public:

Yes, they're in danger, someone better save 'em — yes, they voted Republic.

Frostbite Toast

Stood in the winter heat, call it something like frostbite,

Forever throwing away the bitter me,

Just so we can toast tonight.

Like Wayne said, how can you get the picture if you don't know who
took it?

Saying the one who took it could be the one who's crooked.

Why you think one's still teaching what's in this booklet?

Asking for the proof — it's all around the sky like ashes,

Riding around the country without a roof — yeah, ya boy dashing,

Smashing any witch that wants to corrupt my legion,

Bashing with this switch those ill-intentioned in the region.

Feeling the hate — evidence! Just watch how you grow into your
benevolence.

Baller's Basics

Sitting at the desk, trying to pay attention to the teach,

Still doing the best, even though the brain continues to reach.

Not to become a scholar, more so to show the foundation in becoming a baller.

Oh man, thoughts love to linger,

So go ahead and huddle all around, so we can start to mingle,

Knowing the way this wraps, giving some a tingling sensation,

Dancing so hard you begin to sweat — call it condensation.

With all determination, these threes are just like water,

Ole girl likes the game — yes, it's your daughter.

Everyone knows the name — nope, won't even falter,

Obviously still winning — call it Coach Carter.

Showing how to ball, no need to stand tall,

Paying attention to your own bling, you might see it gleam,

Talking about the ring, or maybe what's within the being.

Germ-Free Hyde

Starting a new job is like parting from an old life,

Becoming rich like Stiller Bob is like trying to find a new wife.

Never trying to commit adultery,

Just trying to sit back and write some more poetry.

So, stay the hell up out this zone — call it truancy,

And if you try and get into my home, one's bringing that army fiercely.

Oh yeah, they are going to punish thee — now call that being germ-free.

That means they are my subject, while they're calling me Dr. Hyde,

Showing you how one is perfect.

Don't even try to run and hide — this ain't no hide and seek.

Come and face one with some pride, before you end up Shit's Creek.

Now see the calming of the tide, enjoying the rest of this marvelous ride.

Crook's Progress

While speaking to this lyric book,

Still contemplating why you think one's something like a crook,

Just trying to find the most efficient way to advance.

Seems to work while they're always swift to get a glance,

Riding this shit so good, you can call it Lance.

Yes, oh so gone, all good, still headstrong,

Showing how to stay in it to win it, just like Armstrong.

Stay looking up, like peering for the horoscope —

What you think we ain't looking down for; we ain't looking through
no microscope.

However, glaring so far with something called a thermal scope,

Step outside and learn to cope with the fear.

More than simple-minded, that's why you're roped up like a deer.

Just enjoy the freedom, as well as this subtle breeze,

Because before planning to meet 'em, must take care of that summer
fling.

Just finished 'em off — it's done, delete 'em.

Knife Grip

Yes, got the joy of life, living it just right,

Hanging on to Betsy — well, that is the knife.

Hope and pray one isn't testy, or it'll happen all tonight.

Why do you think she is looking just so classy,

Being in this ballroom dance, only for the night?

Reaching for the hand, on a chance — best believe it's snazzy,

Taken with another glance, finally making the true stance.

Heaven's Gate

All throughout this life, it feels as though it's been a mistake,

But when receiving that perfect wife, believe in me and take.

Riding like this, being forever straight — nothing like glass, no, we'll never break.

Leaving the old in the past, we're just trying to race to be the first at heaven's gate,

Like zooming by the Atlanta bypass, balling every day, knowing it's my fate.

Blooming straight up out the hole, like a damn rose,

But before grasping the future goal, they're making an ugly pose.

Good thing one's always on the tip... of these damn toes.

Go ahead, create a strategy — seen you shopping at Lowe's,

Banished from thy boundary, especially acting like some hoes.

Secluded Den

Born into a world that seems so full of sin,

As he walks around the family that treats him like the end,

Conjuring enough strength just to pull the win.

Correct — it didn't work, he's just so zealous;

Good thing the Lord works in mysterious ways.

Not being hard to see, some more marvelous days,

So do not try and put the entire world on thy shoulders.

Bet it's way higher than Mt. Everest, still getting colder,

But looking into his eyes, acknowledging he's the bravest.

As the story goes on, you know he got successful,

Even though he's the latest trend, still managed a way to seclude a peaceful den.

Refrain from making him mad, knowing you see the banner,

'Cause when he loses his cool, he turns into the opposite of Bruce Banner.

So don't stick around like a damn fool, 'cause he'll destroy it all — even the damn manor.

Voltron Hustle

The mind is feeling so paralyzed, but don't forget to clean the silver — call it being sterilized.

Being out here trying to eat, even if they want to make a bet — man, just grab the bat.

Start rocking the latest Louis Vuitton — no, you can't wear this hat!

Now, looking up to one like Voltron, hustling — so just take the money, bolt or run.

Yeah, still a youngster, and this feels like the longest yard,

Getting rich like a mobster — better hope one doesn't draw the perfect card,

You just might end up in a dumpster,

Drawing the shortest straw, while spitting these words just so raw.

Yup, they are in the trash — look how these courses clash,

Something like the Titans, while remembering me.

Yes, we always fighting — so consider me.

Crucified Justice

One is always seeking justice,

Won't ever stop until everything is justified.

And if they're hanging from their wrist,

It seems like they were crucified.

So, while talking business, just enjoy a cup of Brisk.

Yeah, this shit is classified — hand over the Bible to testify.

Never rest or lie, while sipping on Corona,

Show your best or die, still tripping on Feona.

Not even trying to cry, but at least they warn ya.

While counting up extra, just listen to this lecture,

Searching in the world for the perfect texture.

You might even think it's something already wrote,

Love to see the look in your eyes, so no need to hope.

Just cope with the fear, and try not to shed a tear.

Best believe that's when they see you, really wanting to come near.

SR-22 Echoes

Why so glued to the TV, B?

Bet they still trying to find a way to emanate me.

Go ahead, suck a cock — me, just dashing by on this Nighthawk!

Keeping that SR-22, they thinking about insurance, cool.

But BRB, 'cause ya boy ain't even reached 22.

Kill a pair of them that's stalking for the substance, oou,

By pulling the hammer back on that SR double-two.

Not trying to be too explicit, just saying, one can fix it.

Going back in time like a looper —

Sorry for the delay in laughter, but this is no blooper.

Always guarding the starship, but not the last trooper,

While steady going through all this hardship,

By seeing it here and viewing it near — yes, one goes the hardest.

Championship Woes

Coming to you like a damn raven,

Call 'em something like Ray Lewis,

Doing it just so bravely,

Keep praying to the God that's close to Jewish.

Yes! They are going to win this tough championship,

Everybody knows it will be like going through a rough relationship.

Being on another floor, or it can be called another level,

Stay fighting off them demons, like they were the devil.

So, you can say, going to the marker, or headed to the target,

Easier than playing soccer — best believe one's going to guard it,

A job given to a goalie,

Appeared, standing all alone, counting on one solely.

While smelling the aroma of the cologne,

Punching ill intent out, 'cause it's way too phony.

Island Bonfire

Praying to the Lord, OMG, knowing what one sees in Thee,

Embodying this desire that others really admire,

Thinking three moves ahead, you can even say one's thinking prior.

Being a girl's BF with this EF, yea, the eternal fire,

Killing new arrivals, leaving them suicidal,

Having to get all inside them,

Betting this plan will not backfire,

We are already on this island,

Smoking next to the bonfire.

So, go ahead and retire, continuously wielding the power,

Cowards really trying to acquire the truth,

Already rolled back the roof,

Wanting to get where we're at, you must provide some proof.

Already told ya, I am the truth!

Still in the face, looking for a physical handout,

Be careful what you ask for, having something non-visible that makes a crowd fan out.

They are still in denial, come and see this walking proof,

It's airborne, yea, viral, tossing it around because it is the loot.

Appearance so ill, you would swear one's walking in a gown, oh please don't frown.

Just here telling my story, with what's approaching, becoming the new glory.

Cliff of Thoughts

Yes, you reap what you sow,

No wonder why it's terrible to look through what your eyes show,

Perhaps easy when it's a deep sleep or dream,

Until reality smacks you in the face, now that's deep shit, it seems.

Strike another match to blow a little more of that short-term please,

Due to how the world is going, might need more than just weed,

Everyone wishing they could jump off a cliff, with wings,

Fly away from all the problems, pulling in a temporary ease,

Absorb all the substance, until you start to hurl,

Not exchanging it for nothing, yes, the verb it's what you yearn.

Telling haters not to approach, before they realize they made a wrong turn!

Trying to find my love, that's controlled by a tight-fitting glove,

When revealed, don't proceed, to show one doesn't intend to mislead,

Take the hand, concede, it's more than a "to be continued."

More like having your top picks on life's expandable menus!

Frozen Action Figures

Seems as though it's inevitable to fill this gaping void with,

Time to be a little more credible, so you're never being toyed with.

Nothing like an action figure, so don't try to configure these actions,

When the body starts to take a frozen look, bet others aren't far behind with a similar outlook.

Why do you think we're always trying to wage war for protection?

Nah, it's like these people want to rage some more.

Correction! Why are they still locking and disappearing talented beings in cages for?

Hmm. Speculation—it makes the world into better places.

Then tell me why we're still going through bullshit cases.

Don't even fix your lips if voicing something that could die,

Like some politicians, having a choice: lie or fly.

They stay looking out for their own skin.

That mindset makes this hand want to take another hit of that wax pen.

First thing on their mind: look, it's tax season.

Trust, and we'll be fine. Yup, that's this evening.

Summer's Chill

This body is so cold, even though it's summer in the world,

Feeling as though they got it on hold, still steady trying to pull the damn cord.

The only thought on her mind is the current home,

So why still worry about me and what's going on?

Blatantly in your face, but you made your choice,

Uncertainty like in space, alas, hearing your voice.

Now you're building your faith; instead, you start to rejoice,

Because you're beginning to feel safe,

Haunted by the memories from back then,

While she's snapping pics, just to ask when.

Smoking double-stuffed until she's high and damn stupid,

Why you think our love is high like Cupid?

Even if it's wicked, frigid, and fucking vivid,

Still always committed, you dimwitted fucking critic.

Nothing like Vin Diesel, but coming at you like Riddick,

Ban keeping it civil, seeing you start to grizzle, but me, just keeping it rizzle.

Parliament of Feelings

These thoughts that just keep lingering in the head,

Seem to come true late at night, while laying in bed.

You have no idea, missing yo ass tremendously.

Wouldn't be in this predicament,

If only saying those three letters… Yes! Instantly.

It feels as though these feelings are going through parliament,

But since they failed to make you rise,

One surmises that they will start to go dormant.

Oh! And continuing to torment,

Saying you miss your best friend, and to rub your tummy.

Go ahead and rest here, forever being a snow bunny.

Remember the long nights back when we were younger?

Yeah, we never stayed sober,

Still steady wanting to lay on this damn shoulder,

Treating ya ass like a shipment,

Ain't even justifying off the right predicament.

Just be satisfied, off this sensible quick pic.

Pandora's Fate

It's so hard to describe, this agonizing pain,

Like Mary Jane and legalizing it, yet so contained.

Hell yeah, they are putting up these cold fronts,

No wonder why these people begin to make it their damn home front.

Maybe they need some guidance,

They could even read about science,

But this uncredible dude wants an alliance.

Couldn't even come close to becoming a client,

Accepting his bait,

Certainly, it will sink, like sealing your fate.

Knowing you like the way that syncs,

But the pain that's caused by every kiss

Drains a bit of life, starting from thy lips.

Six years, your chance, but just a little glance.

No faith in me, and yet you still want to dance

Around the idea of being with me.

It seems you didn't want to consider your keep.

What are you scared of, fearing what's within me?

Telling you, one cared! Forget about the tears that appear on me.

Once they start to become frozen,

You can say the door of feeling stays closed.

We could go all night about the different versions,

But if we keep talking about my heart, go ahead and request the surgeon.

Definitely don't mean to start merging the lock,

Everyone knows, one's stubborn like an ox.

Nope, it ain't budging, until the emergence from Pandora's box.

Shielded Heart

Yes, always follow your heart, even traveling all through the dark

Don't know how much longer these feelings can wait,

Even though it feels as if they're starting to deteriorate.

Everyone says believe and have some faith,

Haven't waited nearly as long as you, but it feels too late.

The magic is making its delay,

It's tragic, but steadily slipping away.

Lord, help me please, so one can contain this fate,

Proclaiming what's really mine, to dictate.

Not meaning to speak of her like property,

But she'll be protected, like she's the crop for me.

Don't try and Sherlock Holmes this mystery,

'Cause you'll never unlock our homes with this chemistry.

Death con five, and they're still trying to slide,

While nosediving for the nine, showing how these bullets collide.

For me, they will see, one protects mine.

Lady in the Frame

All these chicks saying that they're nothing like what one claimed,

Seeing they are just the same as the last one bagged.

While you're trying to cram that picture in the little frame,

Standing here like, it's such a shame

That he's the one you chose, after all the time you put into the game.

Strung you along so much, now you seem to have changed,

And the heart that one wished to obtain

Seems lost forever, within a short little range.

Is that mind so deranged? Even in understanding what's been done, but still won't change.

Shit, our mindset was the only thing that exchanged.

Still, wanting one to wear this heart up on the sleeve. Man, one's outraged!

Rearranged these lyrics on this page, showing you were the item one wanted to seize.

With the interchange of these lines, meant you were the girl one wanted to please.

While listening to these rhymes, it's not hard to tell, you were the one for this creed.

It's hard to ask Mother Hen how much one must endure,

But by the way one comprehends, it's not much longer, that's for sure.

Poured these feelings in this hourglass, and time's about to run out.

Decide before it shatters fast, and in time for one to burn out.

Fuck the one not trying to make it last, they just looking for a timeout.

About-face to the past, 'cause they ain't listening to what's coming out of my mouth!

Great Tribulation

Guess we need something like a Great Tribulation,

'Cause the way we walk around aimlessly seems like we have no regulation.

Yes, they need a mentor, call it a big brother,

But the mind took a detour, seeking one's mother.

Had her qualities but never seen her face-to-face,

Even her personality—now that's a wicked case-to-case.

Fam needs some help, float them into the zone,

So they can begin to have something like comfort in their home.

Slanging drugs in life is not the only way to hustle,

Open your heart and pray to the Father, providing one the muscle.

While asking for a quick pic of your roses,

Can tell that they're dying, like the love when a beat is flowing.

Had one waiting, idling, in these ridiculous poses.

Now unsatisfied, 'cause look who started growing.

Bet this life is classified, not sorry, still yet to see,

Replying with "Take it easy, Q," but it's clear, still won't get the view.

Poured all feelings in this stew, still no comprende with this brew.

Sad seeing you fade away from the crew,

One overcame the past by taking that ass to the Lou.

When over and done with the last, still got to pass the clue.

Trauma to Triumph

After all the time put into helping one recognize,

Thinking one's just going to take it for granted, leaving your ass traumatized.

Going back as far as a trailer, even further to the projects,

Now up in this layer, trying to create new subjects.

Missing mom—could be why one's going through so much trauma,

But staying away from the drama by counting all those commas.

Now distancing thyself from the world,

Becoming more persistent when reaching for the goal,

Loving to make all smile for the rest of my existence,

Living life, but not too proud, keeping up, being consistent.

Too bad if one acts, oh so resistant, just guarding the way to the heart's damn entrance.

The mind keeps racing, like striving for a title, call them the Indiana Pacers,

Or maybe even faster—go speed racer.

Getting to the money, calling it a premium rush,

Yes, they are all appalled, meaning on hush.

Oh, yeah, look at them all, starting to blush,

Showing my happily ever after,

Not trying to be rude, it's just the fact of the matter.

That's why one's always smiling, surrounded by laughter.

Cosmic Shaman

As much as one has already smoked,

One keeps trying to inform that this rooster will never croak.

Failed to accept one at the worst, be prepared to roast,

Everyone can see wanting one at the best,

But the way that glimmers will put your ass to rest.

While tears run down your face,

One's in another altitude, call it space.

Please, do not chase, requiring all this space,

Becoming more valuable, envisioning that extravagant place.

At the same time, looking for a magnificent base,

Or a place to call home, while staying in this zone.

Walking through a storm, thicker than one's own bones.

Life goes on, thanking the world for Tupac,

Now obtaining two Glocks, for a strife-filled world.

Ill manners approaching the door, be prepared to pay the toll,

Or else get folded—no, ain't talking about clothes.

Just trying to reach my peak, yeah, then behold!

Even while haters still mooching, looking for a handout,

Use the vocals in an instant, and watch them all pan out.

While crying out like Mario, just go pro,

Record another hero like Dan Marino.

Rocky Toll

Feeling so painful, with emptiness and despair,

Always being sensible, with readiness and no compare.

Why they always down me, like they know everything?

You can never clown me, since the surpass of my only claim.

They couldn't make it stick; they never saw me at the scene,

Running miles through the twigs, still coming out clean.

Had to drop stacks on a lawyer, saying, "Stay out of court,"

Still trying to be a grower, even in the damn north.

Please tell me why, so obligated to this lifestyle?

Maybe it's regulated through this life for miles.

Trying to find the joy that is in the future,

Worrying about the torment that haunts this feature.

No longer being toyed with because of my presence,

Now stop looking at me, like a peasant!

Don't want to pull my crescent, ain't talking about the roll,

Yes, it's an axe, in case they want to turn up to the max.

Don't make me mix you up like some rocky road,

Sending you down that rocky road.

Caring less about your cocky hold,

One even scolds his own, so how are you going to pay the toll?

Phantom Wrath

More like an entertainer in what they say is a godforsaken world,

Not for laughs or gimmicks,

But from what's taken and curled around.

In the past life, one was somebody else's wrath, their mimic.

However, the tables have turned, being the reflection of the walking pain.

Thought this time would be different, once the mind, body, and soul were in the equation.

But the misleading deceits, from rigorous defeats,

Have shown the path that many must meet.

When hit with a conclusion, no medicine can treat.

This is all random, but more so like a gamble, no, not starting to ramble.

So, inform why one's constantly reminded of this phantom.

Can't get it out the head, this burnt image in the skull,

The actions that were taken seem like this existence should've been null.

Even had a heart to heart, but little hints said one was told,

"Listen to the harp, cover your heart, use a tarp, and leave her ass alone."

Looks can be deceiving, love is a stronger feeling,

And that's now what one is receiving, not a conclusion to our sealing.

Her actions are always showing two different sides,

Like a coin, two-faced, living two different lives.

Half of her body wants our lives to be intertwined,

When the other half wants one out of her mind.

Now she is preaching to start anew,

Choosing in the moment how to forget, was drinking this shine till becoming blue.

Loving you too much, for you to want to kill yourself.

Was willing to make this work, but our bond was made on a bed full of lies.

Except my love, it reaches taller than the highest bookshelf,

But how can one trust you again when our past life flashed before my very eyes?

Tragic Saturday

Maybe true love is not for me.

No matter what's done or given, they all seem to leave me be.

Giving all to the one of my dreams, as she falls into another boy's arms,

Still seeing her in the mind, memories, even streams,

Struggling to knock down her walls, even with this charm.

She built them back up; might as well have been left behind bars.

The greatest fear happened—it ended in a tragedy.

Walking in on it, just this Saturday.

How could we be so close together, while still missing your touch?

Saying we will be like this forever, despite trying to fix it in a rush.

Future plans started to crumble when you started seeking attention from others.

Gave you many chances to avoid the stumble,

But you still made love to that fucking turner.

Thinking you and your body were mine, like an owner,

And mine yours instead of a burner.

Continued to try and fix us, with this heart maimed.

Finding promises and words to him that you told caused even more pain.

Was wanting you to be the one, while being the one,

Instead of a stepping stone, skipping to the next block.

The door came unlocked, you sleeping hard as a rock.

Happy, even comfortable—call me slappy the dummy, just so vulnerable.

Wish there was a way to see this coming,

But how could I when you're exclaiming, you didn't want to lose me?

It's like your words were trying to move me,

But in the opposite direction,

Wanting only to stay in your section.

Loving you even after all that you've done, still wanted to make it work.

Just needed to know, are the boys still going to lurk,

Or should I end it now, by jumping off this fort?

Witchdoctor's Curse

With every waking breath, it seems like another step toward this demise.

Still climbing out of bed, but to find death

Not only in the eyes, but also in the mind.

Tearing the heart and brain apart, like a divide and conquer,

When really, just wanting the doctor.

Making promises to always be by this side,

Cherokee in her, so call her the witchdoctor, even moving the tide.

Must've put one under a spell, unable to get out, oh, so compelled.

Saying one can't love—maybe it's after you, trying to solve what we were,

But so one-sided, putting in all the work.

Maybe it's because you lost faith and love in us,

Having no regrets, loving the lust.

So why still talk, acting like this is what you want?

Are you trying to find which of us can play the part,

So you can finally cut one off?

Why can't you be honest, when I never lied?

Show me you're still modest, and I can show you how he died.

Just return to being my goddess.

Being in this aura must've changed the person I fell in love with,

'Cause who I talked to every day was replaced—it wasn't real, like a myth.

She was the one I wanted to walk to the end of the earth with,

The one I wanted until the end of time, like a perfect soul,

One who could've melted this heart of gold,

For this payphone, using the last dime

To tell you, not even this crooked smile could change our lives from the final countdown.

Yes, one thing to take from this dying body on the ground

Is that you had undying love—true love—from the one in ten thousand who came around.

Hermit Habit

Trying to forget this pain in a flash,

Started drinking when awoken, every day.

It would be so much easier with a bag of hash,

Just speaking the truth, per se.

Still reaching for the top, trying to keep the mind right,

Never trying to flop, but clearing the mind tonight.

Finding other ways, getting ahead, off the situation at hand.

Had to go into isolation, just to be able to cope.

The only reminder was how we were going to elope,

Taking seven days just to make a habit.

Since no more communication, marking that on the tablet.

But getting off track, time to get back to the fact

That the time away is showing me who I am.

Time to get out of the dump & start glowing from these rhymes.

And pretty much thank you, to now realizing one's true ties,

That if it wasn't for the end, true life wouldn't begin, keeping the chin treading water,

And writing lines till these pages end. When making it to the top, don't think it's for you.

Other people in the world are struggling with this too.

There's a way to come out of this dark past, dark home,

Find something in you to make it last, make it whole, and stray from being alone.

With a ray of sunlight on your face, it makes it hard to delay

What's really coming in this space, bringing happiness to convey.

Walking this earth is still the best case,

So don't try to switch it to the old place.

Phoenix Resurrection

Used to smoke a lot to forget all the past memories,

Now I put the pen on this paper and remember thee.

Walking through this world, to visualize a better future,

But getting cut down at the waist,

Makes it harder to realize the bigger picture.

However, by crawling out of the waste, surely you'll get to a better place.

Just know every great comeback starts with a fallback.

Pick yourself up, and don't forget your club hat,

Keep walking around with your head up, getting chased by pussy cats.

Continue following that inclined hill

And watch how these nations' religions combine with free will

To the truth that is speaking underneath the field.

That's the holy ground one walks upon, to a temper that's getting ill.

That's an old soul's desire, heaven on earth being fulfilled.

And what transpired is that I am bringing it here,

With love as the power, this authenticity sets the stage aqui.

And with it within he, so when the world sees thee,

They will praise that the spirit is within me.

Heaven on Earth

Gazing into your eyes is like a journey through the soul,

Climbing Machu Picchu to the brink,

To truly find what your core really seeks.

Glancing backstage even for a peek,

Leaves one overwhelmed in bliss, with seeds to be reaped.

Don't look down or back at the old life to weep,

Stand your ground, with a crown,

To see heaven on earth, the life He has given you to keep.

Don't be faint,

After He has given you the power to become a saint.

Use the whole gallon of color,

With Thy brush, given you the city to paint.

Don't be late,

For the dinner prepared for you, that most would call fate.

Close your eyes, go within, and see the light,

Open your eyes, gaze at the stars, and see the outer light that shines
brightly in the night.

Sing the pink farewell, that's a link to a Nightingale tale.

Although Thy knees may be weak,

Remember He gives strength to those full of faith, which are meek.

Soul's Depths

How deep does one soul go?

Beneath the roots, of the roots, or like a dream within a dream?

Embedded in your DNA, solemn truth!

Or let it wash away, like a rainy day.

Come unto me, my darling Ruth! To see this very essence is the startling truth.

Walk this road alone, but don't forebode. Sorrow-filled clone, put to your control.

Only through love can they patrol,

Your true heart's desire, between these two worlds.

So there's no need to conspire upon this divine union marriage.

There's no compare, nor power

To the temptations that test, which become devoured.

Would even settle down, Quagmire, just to admire this 5D empire.

All praise to the Most High, yes His way!

Do you actually think one walked this weary borrowed road, all alone, without the Omega to really thank every day? Silly soul!

Source runs through these veins,

For the divine will's claim,

To show it's not, no damn game.

Bend the knee for your free will to keep,

Show these enemies how there can be a friend in me,

But only if thy eye is keen,

To the true knowledge that beams

Through to the silver sandwich that gleams.

Since the divine's will is the last thread to this seam.

Incantation of Unity

Staring at another has one fighting their own reflection,

While looking at each other to inspire,

Can help shed transgressions.

Follow one like Longmire,

Can show the one, if he may, a star show, star shower.

How powerful thy words when saying incantation, through a skewed perspective of power,

To show who are the true cowards,

With the intentions of wholeness, unity.

One's fears alter to oneness, purity.

With words that cure the nations, starting within small communities,

Search within, go within.

Yes, that word will show the light unto thee again,

To the path which was darkened, to that reflection at the beginning, my friend.

Allow the spirit to guide one through the nature of this rhyme,

And use your own perspective, open the eyes.

And with the will of the divine, now seeing who's creating the true crime,

Of the essence, no time to waste.

That sensational presence, and the signs, one will chase,

The coming of the Lord, His word, one will embrace.

Magnetic Tea

Channeling through these hands, call one a scribe now,

Going with the ebb & flow, with a pet white crow.

While road running around bands, just for show,

Stay close, with true soul clan, to help awaken that holy ghost.

With unconditional love, as the true heart's plan,

Then can one see thee, the spirit within, that will never leave thee.

Sit down, with a cup of green tea, while staying in the present, to get the real tea,

To show how one is so magnetic to the truth, that shall set one free.

With a soul older than the park of Jurassic,

A warm smile that makes one feel oh so fantastic, while curing the masses.

But one must subtract and not let the mind get carried away.

This could be abstract to ye, with little faith, under the Milky Way.

Yes, one will contrast all those who oppose the will of the one who sent thee,

But not before closing doors and healing, with love and a rose.

That takes commitment, with a truth sealing; do not worry, these words are poised,

Chosen carefully to cut through the noise.

Arise, wake up from the dormant slumber,

To see the ones who are no longer encumbered.

God-Given Loot

What one really wants is to express this significant message,

Channeling from higher truths, that leaves one with a courageous lesson.

These actions seen with honest proof, for the unbridled scoop

That you cannot take, God-given loot.

Told ye, that one speaks the truth,

The words that they speak with fleeting attempts

Made one release the sin.

It should be words that one keeps, with no surrender or tempt.

The conspiracy of the old skin,

Knock the dust off your chin, with a flick of the pen.

One's patience will turn their reward into ten,

Diligently seeking, the one raising above true sin.

Control one's mind, while continuing to climb,

Meditating in nature helps reveal the nature of the divine,

With hearts truly aligned,

One sees the lecture of the purpose behind deciphering this rhyme.

Cold Spoon

Lost mom before one could hold a spoon to these words,

Didn't even get a chance to see her face,

Feeling so alone in this world,

Still looking for her without a trace.

Going through a bitter earth, trying not to stumble,

Contemplating what this life is worth, still ending in a fumble.

Is there something that it lacks,

Even though this motivation is striving to the front like a running back?

Maybe karma has its own continuous plan,

The drama that one sees is worse than the vengeance plan.

Confused through this dark night,

Or should one say tasked with an impossible choice, like the Dark Knight—

Saving someone you love, or leaving thy heart to burn,

'Cause that one that you love will leave your ass at the first turn!

Setting puzzle pieces together, and they won't fit,

Check with your intuition, let's see if it was the wrong turn!

Please, don't tell one something that's unfathomable grit,

Like putting eggs and grits on the table—that's something one won't eat.

Gambling on life like one already had the fix,

But with this faith, he brought me the finest dish.

Pristine Life

Was it the presence that eludes from awareness,

Or is it the silence that concludes from being stylish?

For one speaks, and ye do not see,

For ye listen, and yet have sight.

How can thee fathom what one says,

Yet still not know thyself?

Multiple planes, and multiple selves,

Pick the heart's choice with the reins.

A couple of atoms, fighting aspects of self,

Rise to a higher plan, to see what's abundant with health.

Clearly not going insane, just alchemizing the pain,

Throwing dirt on thy name, just to traumatize thy lane.

Keep the Most High, never fall to those karmic things,

Aim the vibe to the sky, to see past those tragic ties.

Claim the tribes that never die,

While revealing shit still attracts flies.

Don't stay content with what you perceive,

Ye with little faith must be grateful, and it wouldn't hurt to say please.

Because once submitted, one's reality will change the scene,

To the heart's desire, with wedding rings.

No fighting over power, for we know He will seize,

And cause a damn tower that can bring all to their knees.

So enjoy the good life, which all will see as so damn pristine.

Invisible Cord

All one felt was the core of the emotion,

No spoken word, due to the power of this deduction,

With a true connection that will never corrode,

That's a pure poker hand that will never fold.

The energy flows like a visible cord,

To not forget the origin of our role.

The unjust will see what glows from this invisible world,

The just will see home, realizing heaven on earth is the true goal.

As our hands engage, feeling the love that solves all pain,

Picking up the dove as we follow the chain,

Respect to the one above before we proclaim,

Mother Gaia, it's done, you are now self-made.

The flow of this intention warms the hearts of those who listen.

Energy goes where you commit it; observe the situation, oh no, don't forget it.

Bruce Lee's Roots

What is experienced is what is seen, the roots from creation, at the top of the tree.

Go ahead, ask the sirens for another confirmation, then one will be free

From the crooks of damnation—just kick 'em like Bruce Lee.

The seeds that are planted in the ground, what we call the subconscious,

Now sprouting from thee crown—no, no, not unconscious.

No doubting, open thy eyes,

But start thinking consciously and use some damn caution.

Due to the fact the thought is the water,

To bring forth what has been brought, nourishing thy garden.

One now is freed from the emotional catastrophe,

Yes, that tree flourishing above thy enemies.

Oh, one knows it can be seen, what's been mothered in that tree,

Whether good or bad, knowing what was planted in thee.

With the vibration of these tones,

Remember to always seek the highest pole,

For one to project what your inner has controlled.

The sensation that you get will resonate, throughout the bones.

Now don't forget the power one controls.

Cycles of Ascension

Going through life's cycles,

As if running around the track.

Don't trash memories, just recycle,

To ascend from what ye lack.

Knowing oneself is truly vital,

From what's projected unto the title.

That's the life all really admire,

But it draws cowards to these false idols.

Transcend past all these petty desires,

Like a phoenix that is rising above the ashes.

From within, you will see what is your passion.

Pay no attention to those with fake eyelashes.

All they do is impose what really needs some traction.

Reflect to them the ALL to show what's the real attraction.

Compose the heart into gold, praise the little whisper that told

How to unlock one's soul, that's yearning to come home.

Heighten the awareness to the present,

Yes, this presence is what one cherishes.

No comparison to what has perished—

Open your eyes to see the present.

Seeds of Bliss

Being told not to hold the world on these shoulders,

Alas, that fight will show how the world is internal.

With might, one can push down those boulders,

But with sight, seeing what's projected is external.

The thoughts to these seeds are the water that fills the streams,

Caught up in another's creed, surely it seems extreme.

Keep giving in peace to the unseen, now living with bliss in the waking dream.

Deep down inside, look, see! Full of gold,

Rush to the other side and feel the story unfold.

Smiling and climbing as this starlight keeps shining,

Adore dancing with Vita, and one will see how it's just so bonita.

Even with lips sealed, yet not the story untold,

Brace yourself, it's unsealed, they acknowledge how ye rose

Through the valley of the shadows, and yet He still shows the passage to the rose.

Divine Dance

The dance with the Divine is so subtle, yet sublime.

The inner glance of what's inside can cuddle when combined.

The guide with the true heart walks the path that shines.

What they call a trance is no illusion nor chance,

More like a grand plan, that's the solution, no delusion.

Slowing down the physical with the imagination, that's just so mystical,

Helps one reflect back the true nature of life's miracle.

With a gentle release from within,

Is the breath, as on the surface, the wind.

Feel, listen, follow the whistle,

With love in the heart, stronger than any tenfold missile.

As the mirror, we are illuminating, showing what is seeking,

We anchor in what we know to be amiss,

While seeing eternal bliss that has commenced.

Ascended Flame

For the one who isn't known, to the one who is forever shown,

The path to release the fear, so the stream may shed a tear,

Rather for joy or pain,

Either way, they bring the same,

Knowledge to set thy eyes on the eternal gaze,

Of what's to appear, quicker than a lighter's flame.

Truly, unto you it is said,

The one who diligently seeks will gain

The understanding of what is to be reclaimed,

That's close to you, like a lion's mane.

Child, follow the flames of the Ascended Masters,

Thy ember will ignite, as a fulfilled maestro,

Gaining inner strength, like a man on a tightrope.

Taking this leap will show how much one gives hope,

Knowing what this means, go ahead and bend the knee,

Now donning the crown, so one truly leads.

www.ingramcontent.com/pod-product-compliance
Lightning Source LLC
Chambersburg PA
CBHW051325120626
46547CB00015B/2400